Celtic Warrior

the legend of Cú Chulainn

Chapter One

COURAGE

AFTER OLIVER SHEPPARD

40 days beforehand, at the southernmost tip of Ireland.
Cú Chulainn
HA!, HE IS BUT ONE MAN.
A LONE WARRIOR AT THE SUMMIT OF IRELAND.
YET HE CHOOSES TO STAND AGAINST THE ENTIRE ARMY OF MAEVE.
I'LL GLADLY BET ALL OF MY LAND THAT I COULD TAKE HIM OUT BY MYSELF.
THOSE WOULD BE BRAVE WORDS, FIACHA IF YOU WERE THE OWNER OF MORE THAN A SIMPLE PIG FARM.
HAHA, MAYBE SO, BUT I WILL LAY CLAIM TO A LOT MORE THAN THAT ONCE I SLIT THE BOY'S THROAT.
AND BESIDES, I HEAR PIGS ARE EXACTLY THE KIND OF COMPANY YOU LIKE TO KEEP AT NIGHT!
CLEARLY, MY OLD FRIEND, YOU HAVE NEVER HEARD THE STORIES ABOUT THE YOUNG HOUND OF ULSTER.
SHUNK

WE WILL *LEVEL* HIS MOUNTAINS, *BURN* HIS FORESTS AND *PLUNDER* HIS WOMEN.

AND IN DOING SO WE WILL BURY *ANY* MEMORIES AND TALES OF THE ONE WHO DARES STAND UP AGAINST OUR QUEEN.

SO TAKE YOUR DRINK IN YOUR HAND. ENJOY YOUR NIGHT.
TOMORROW WE CROSS THE PLAINS OF IRELAND, TO CLAIM DONN CŪAILNGE, THE BROWN BULL OF ULSTER, AND ITS LANDS FOR MAEVE.
FOR MAEVE

FOOLS, THEY KNOW NOT WHAT THEY FIGHT FOR, YET THEY CHEER WITH ALL THEIR HEARTS.

AND NO MAN SHALL BE SPARED UNTIL I TAKE IT.
from 300 miles away
across the whole of ireland.
ARRRROOOOHHHHHH

WHAT WAS THAT?
FIACHA, MY FRIEND, WAKE UP!
MMM
OLD MAN, WHAT MAKES YOU WAKE ME FROM MY SLEEP?
I HEARD SOMETHING OUTSIDE.
YOU WHAT?
IM TELLING YOU, I HEARD THE HOWL OF AN EVIL BEAST!

GET YOUR REST. WE SET OFF AT DAWN.

FINE, I'LL GO LOOK BY *MYSELF*.

HO THERE! GUARDS.

ON YOUR PATROLS, DID YOU PERHAPS HEAR ANYTHING OUT OF THE ORDINARY? I COULD SWEAR I HEARD A ROAR COMING FROM OUTSIDE THE SETTLEMENT.

DRINKING TOO MUCH, ARE WE, SOLDIER? THERE IS NOTHING TO BE HEARD HERE OTHER THAN THE SNORING OF THOUSANDS OF *DRUNKEN MEN*.
PERHAPS THE LITTLE MAN HAD A *NIGHTMARE?*
HAHA! THE *HOUND OF ULSTER* IS COMING TO GET HIM IN HIS SLEEP!

YOU'RE ABSOLUTELY SURE?

LOOK, GET BACK INTO YOUR DWELLING BEFORE I...

ROOWAAR
WARRIORS OF IRELAND AWAKEN! WE ARE UNDER ATTACK!

GRRRGH!
RRAARGH!
THESE ARE NO HOUNDS. THEY ARE POSSESSED BEASTS!
RAGHHR
BACK! BACK TO HELL WITH YOU.

RRRGH
RUN FOR YOUR LIVES.

SHLUCKT

ANY MAN WHO FLEES WILL HAVE TO ANSWER TO ME.

I AM CORMAC CONNLOINGES AND I WILL HUNT YOU DOWN AND TAKE YOUR HEAD AS A PRIZE, LIKE I WILL WITH THESE HOUNDS.

KILL
THEM ALL.
SVVITH
CLUNKTH

NEVER BEFORE HAVE I SEEN HOUNDS AS FEROCIOUS AS THESE.
I HAVE. ONE GUARDED THE COURT OF MY FATHER, KING CONCHOBAR BEFORE I WENT INTO EXILE.
THESE ARE CŪ CHULAINN'S HOUNDS.
ulster, the court of conchobar mac nessa
13 years ago.
THWACK

THUNK
DON'T EVEN THINK ABOUT IT, BOY.
HAHAHA! I LIKE THIS ONE, CULAINN.
HOLD STILL, YOU SCRAPPY LITTLE...
hahaha
AS DO I, CONCHOBAR, AS DO I.
UUUMMPH!
FFUMP

THAT AND HE JUST KICKED A KING IN THE GUT.

HAHA, THAT TOO. COME WITH ME AND I WILL FEED YOU AND SEE YOU GET A BED FOR THE NIGHT.

I TELL YOU, THE GOAL MY BOY SCORED TODAY WAS ONE WORTHY OF THE FIELDS OF TARA THEMSELVES. ISN'T THAT RIGHT, YOUNG CORMAC?
AND I HAVE NO DOUBT THAT WITH A BIT OF TRAINING, THIS YOUNG SETANTA HERE WILL BE A FINE SPORTSMAN HIMSELF.
TELL ME, BOY, HOW DO YOU FARE WITH A HURLEY AND A SLIOTHAR?
IF YOU PROVE YOURSELF SKILFUL ENOUGH THEN MAYBE YOU CAN DWELL IN THIS CASTLE FOR LONGER AS ONE OF THE MEMBERS OF MY TEAM.
THE HURLEY TAKES YEARS OF PRACTICE TO MASTER.
KLUNK
BUT IT TAKES FAR MORE THAN SKILL TO PLAY. YOU NEED TO BE BRAVER THAN MOST MEN TO BE THE BEST AT THIS GAME.

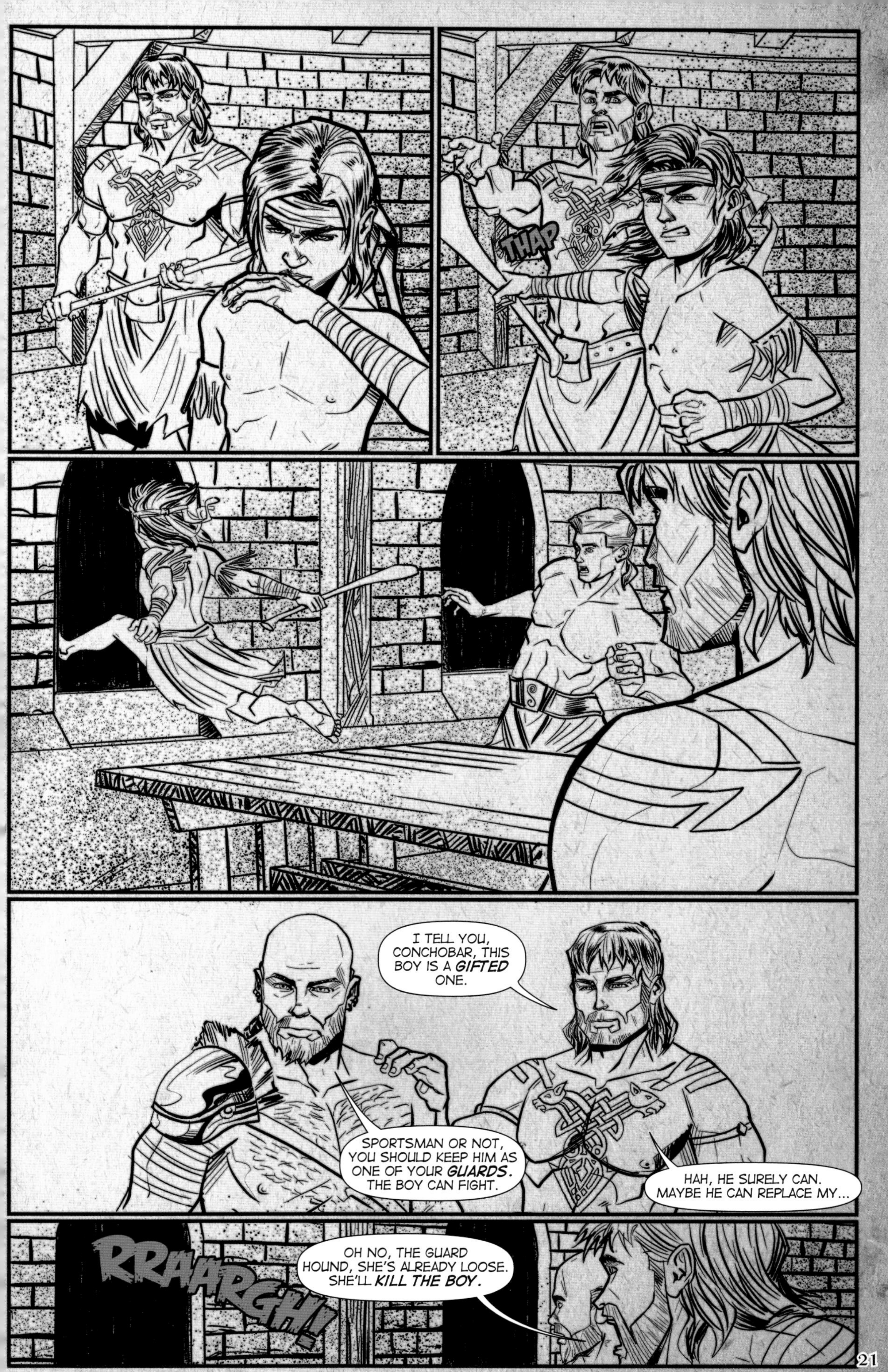
THAP
I TELL YOU, CONCHOBAR, THIS BOY IS A GIFTED ONE.
SPORTSMAN OR NOT, YOU SHOULD KEEP HIM AS ONE OF YOUR GUARDS. THE BOY CAN FIGHT.
HAH, HE SURELY CAN. MAYBE HE CAN REPLACE MY...
RRAAARGH!!
OH NO, THE GUARD HOUND, SHE'S ALREADY LOOSE. SHE'LL KILL THE BOY.

SETANTA! WATCH OUT FOR THE ...

HOUND?

SHE HAS PROTECTED THIS CASTLE FOR YEARS. SHE HAS FENDED OFF HUNDREDS OF INTRUDERS.
YOU, BOY, WILL DO HER JOB FROM NOW ON, UNTIL HER CUBS ARE OLD ENOUGH TO TAKE OVER.
YOU ARE SETANTA NO MORE.
YOU ARE MY HOUND NOW.
THAT IS HOW THE BOY GOT HIS NAME, AS THE HOUND OF CULAINN, - CÚ CHULAINN.
SO THESE ARE HIS HOUNDS?

WE'VE YET TO PASS OUR ***FIRST*** NIGHT, AND NOW OUR ARMY IS DOWN ALMOST ***FIVE HUNDRED*** MEN.

Celtic Warrior

the legend of Cú Chulainn

chapter two

'they root the tree all the way down to the gates of hell themselves
Strength

FERGUS!

FERGUS, I BRING NEWS FROM THE **SOUTH**.

GAH...
I BRING...
PATIENCE, YOUNG **MAC ROTH**, PATIENCE.

EVEN WHEN WE MARCH INTO **WAR**, THERE IS TIME TO **REST**.

TAKE THE TIME TO APPRECIATE THE *BEAUTY* OF THIS ISLAND. KNOW THE LAND THAT YOU WISH TO *CONQUER* FOR YOUR QUEEN.

THEN LET US HOPE THAT, LIKE US, THEY HAVE KEPT THEIR SPIRITS UP.
the Gap of dunloe
YOU'RE CARRYING WHAT?
KEEP IT DOWN, WILL YOU. I DON'T WANT ANYONE ELSE TO FIND OUT.
YOU DON'T WANT ANYONE TO FIND OUT YOU ARE CARRYING YOUR SEVERED ARM AROUND WITH YOU?
YOU DON'T UNDERSTAND... IT'S MY ARM. I CAN'T JUST LET IT GO. WE'VE BEEN THROUGH A LOT TOGETHER.
OH, BELIEVE ME, I UNDERSTAND YOUR FEELINGS, BUT I'VE HAD NO PROBLEM LEAVING BEHIND THE MANY WOMEN WHO HAVE PROVIDED THE SAME DUTIES OF YOUR HAND OVER THE LAST FEW YEARS.

THAT'S NOT WHAT I MEAN AND YOU *KNOW* IT.
OH *REALLY?* THEN *WHAT ELSE* DO YOU WANT TO DO WITH IT?
JUST LET ME BE, WILL YOU.
SHLUMP

THE HOUND OF ULSTER IS MISTAKEN IF HE FEELS A FEW OF HIS PETS CAN FRIGHTEN ME OFF.

BY THE GODS.
HOW IN THE NAME OF ERIU DID AN ASH TREE GET HERE?

IT WAS PUT HERE.

WHAT DO WE DO NOW?
WELL, THE MOUNTAINS ARE TOO STEEP FOR OUR CHARIOTS, AND THOSE ROOTS GO ALL THE WAY UP THE SIDE. BUT WE CAN'T JUST TURN BACK. WE WOULD LOSE WEEKS BY NOT TAKING THIS PASSAGE.

READY YOUR WEAPONS, MEN.

WE'RE TAKING DOWN THAT TREE!

10 YEARS AGO.
IN THREE YEARS, NOT ONLY HAS THAT BOY RAISED MY HOUND'S CUBS, BUT HE HAS BROUGHT IN EVERY WILD DOG FOR MILES AND HAS BECOME THEIR MASTER.
HMMM, A SHAME THEN THAT YOUR DEAL WITH HIM IS ALMOST UP. ANY OF THOSE HOUNDS ALONE IS FIERCE ENOUGH TO PROTECT YOUR HOME.
THAT IS VERY TRUE, MY OLD FRIEND.
CŪ CHULAINN, MY BOY. COME HERE, TO THE THRONE ROOM.
I THINK IT IS TIME YOU TOOK UP ARMS.

REMEMBER, LAD, THAT ONCE YOU TAKE UP A SWORD, YOU WILL DO SO AS A FREE IRISHMAN.
THESE SWORDS ARE FORGED FOR THE RED BRANCH ARMY FROM THE FINEST STEEL OF THE MUIRTHEMNE PLAINS. ONLY THE STRONGEST MEN CAN WIELD THEM.
USE IT ONLY TO DEFEND YOURSELF AND OTHERS, NEVER TO ATTACK.
NEVER LET IT LEAVE YOUR SIDE,
TREAT IT WITH WITH UTMOST RESPECT.
AND BEFORE YOU TAKE ONE,
PROVE YOU CAN USE IT BY CARVING YOURSELF A SHIELD.

AND REMEMBER, WHATEVER YOU DO, STAY AWAY FROM THE ASH TREE. EVEN YOU AREN'T SKILLED ENOUGH TO CARVE IT.
THE OAK TREE GIFTS YOU WITH PROTECTION.
THE HOLLY TREE GIFTS YOU WITH SURVIVAL.
THE HAZEL TREE GIFTS YOU WITH WISDOM.
YEAH, BOY, I BET YOU ARE THINKING EXACTLY WHAT I AM.

THE ASH TREE GIFTS YOU WITH THE SOULS OF IRELAND'S FIERCEST WARRIORS.
ACK!

DIG IN, MEN, GET THAT TREE *UPROOTED*. PULL IT FROM THE *VERY EARTH* ITSELF.
DON'T LET ME GO.
CRAACK
NOOO!

THUUUMP
WE'RE LOSING THIS BATTLE. *RETREAT!*

DO NOT GIVE IN.

DON'T GIVE... ARRRGH!

NOOO!

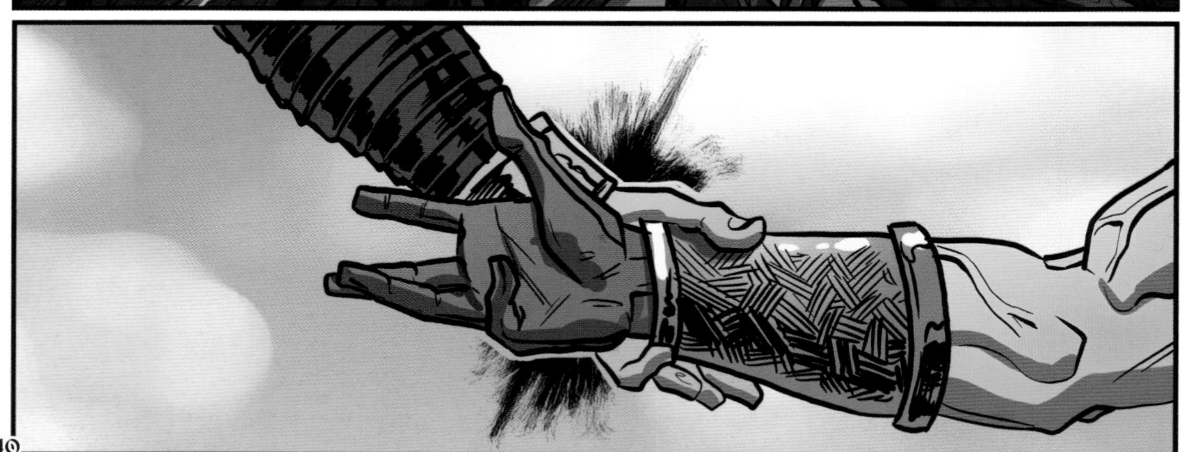

WARRIORS OF THE WEST. ATTTAAACCKKK!
FERGUS?
NNGGHH!
WELL, MY FRIEND, IT APPEARS I HAVE PULLED YOU FROM THE GATES OF HELL ITSELF.
IT LOOKS LIKE I'M NOT THE ONLY ONE FLIRTING WITH ITS DOOR.
THAP
TIME TO CLOSE IT SHUT!

GO FOR THE ROOTS. PULL IT FREE FROM THE SOIL.
IT'S COMING LOOSE.
NOW IS OUR CHANCE. BRING IT DOWN!
KTHOOOOOM

I THOUGHT WE WERE DONE FOR THERE.
IF IT WAS NOT FOR FERGUS'S ARMY COMING TO YOUR AID, WE MAY **VERY** WELL HAVE BEEN.
AND **NOBODY** HAS ANY IDEA HOW IT GOT HERE?

NO GROUP OF MEN, OF **ANY SIZE**, COULD HAVE MOVED **THAT TREE**.
YOU COULD BE RIGHT ABOUT THAT. LOOK AT THE **CARVING UNDERNEATH** IT.

IT SAYS, 'LET NO MAN PASS UNLESS HE HAS THE STRENGTH TO PURGE THIS TREE BY *HIMSELF*.'

BY *HIMSELF?* THIS *CANNOT* BE TRUE?

IT *CAN'T* BE.

IF CÚ CHULAINN DID INDEED PUT THIS TREE HERE BY HIMSELF THEN IT'S NOT JUST HIS STRENGTH WE HAVE TO WORRY ABOUT.

HE COULD VERY WELL BE THE ONLY MAN EVER IN THE *HISTORY* OF *IRELAND*...

TO FIGHT WITH A SHIELD BORN FROM THE ASH TREE ITSELF.

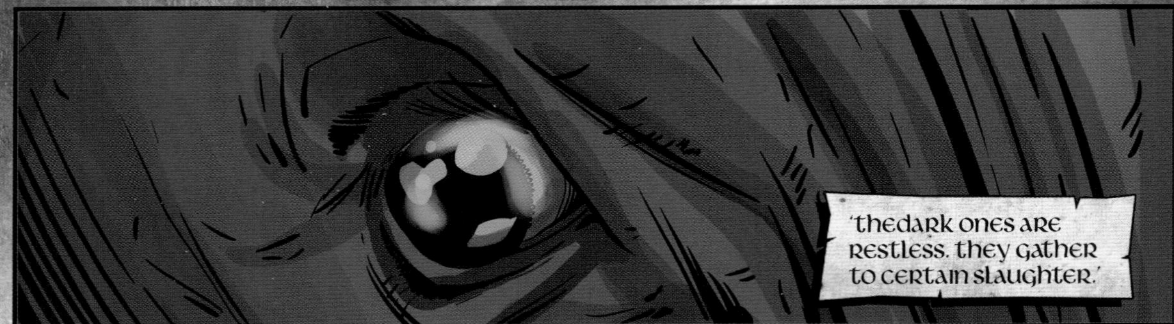

Celtic Warrior

the legend of Cú Chulainn

chapter three

WARRIORS, BRING ME THE BROWN BULL OF ULSTER.
'But what he fights for will live on in Ireland forever.'

destiny

the RIVER shannon
YOU HAVE FACED THE TRIALS OF CŪ CHULAINN,

kilskeer
YOU HAVE LEVELLED HIS FORESTS,

the windy gap of omeath
OPENED UP HIS MOUNTAINS,

the hill of tara, seat of the high king.
AND SLEPT IN HIS OWN LAND.

THOUGH WE HAVE ALREADY LOST MANY, WE KNOW OUR BROTHERS HAVE FALLEN FOR A GREAT CAUSE.
SOME OF YOU SERVE ME FREELY. SOME NEEDED A LITTLE MORE PERSUASION. BUT MY CONTROL OVER ALL OF YOU IS STRONG.
ONLY ONE REALM OF IRELAND REMAINS OUT OF MY CONTROL.
EVEN THERE, ALL BUT ONE OF THE WARRIORS OF THE RED BRANCH ARMY HAVE BEEN CURSED BY A LONG LASTING EVIL. THEY WILL NOT AWAKEN UNTIL THIS BATTLE IS OVER.

THE SYMBOL OF THEIR LAND, DONN CÚAILNGE, THE BROWN BULL OF ULSTER, CANNOT BE TAKEN FREELY. IT WILL BE TAKEN BY FORCE.
UNDER MY ENCHANTMENT YOU WILL BE WITHOUT FEAR, YOU WILL BE WITHOUT REMORSE.
AND WITHOUT YOUR QUEENS,
YOU WILL BE MINE!

ONCE WE PILLAGE OUR ENEMIES' HOMES, NO ONE SHALL MATCH US FOR WEALTH. TOGETHER, WE WILL RULE ALL OF IRELAND.
6 YEARS AGO

COME ON!
UP THERE, IN THE HILLS BEHIND THAT STONE. THAT SHOULD BE SAFE ENOUGH.
STAY HERE NOW. WE DARE NOT GET ANY CLOSER TO A RITUAL OF THE GODS.

I AM AINE, GODDESS OF *HEALING*.
I AM LIR, GOD OF THE *SEA*.
I AM MAEVE, GODDESS OF *INTOXICATION*.
I AM MACHA, GODDESS OF *FERTILITY*.

I SEE IT CRIMSON, I SEE IT RED.
LOOKS LIKE WE'RE JUST IN TIME, TOO.
I SEE A WORLD WHICH WILL NOT BE DEAR TO ME. A SUMMER WITHOUT HARVESTS, THE SEA WITHOUT LIFE.
MEN WITHOUT HEARTS AND WOMEN WITHOUT CHILDREN.
YOU FOUR ARE THE DEITIES OF THESE REALMS. ONE OF YOU IS A BETRAYER, A REAVER TO YOUR OWN, AND AN ENEMY TO YOUR LAND.
AS MORRIGAN, THE GODDESS OF WAR, I MUST KEEP ALL OF THE ELEMENTS IN BALANCE, OR THIS ISLAND WILL FALL INTO CHAOS.
I KNOW THAT ONE OF YOU...
GASP
RAAAAGGH!

DIE, YOU WITCH!
YOU THINK I AM SUCH A FOOL,
THAP
THAT I DO NOT KNOW AN ACT OF SORCERY WHEN I SEE IT.
ACK!
THAT THE GODDESS OF WAR DOES NOT KNOW WHEN SHE IS BEING PLAYED!

YOU ARE A POWERFUL GODDESS, MAEVE, BUT DON'T LET YOUR ARROGANCE BLIND YOU. YOUR INTOXICATIONS DO NOT WORK ON ALL MEN.
IT'S NOT JUST THE MEN YOU HAVE TO WORRY ABOUT.
WHAT?
SHLIICCK
EAAASY, BOY.

I TOO SEE IT CRIMSON. FINNBENNACH, THE WHITE HORNED BULL IS MINE. ONCE DONN CÚAILNGE OF ULSTER HAS FALLEN, ALL OF IRELAND'S CHILDREN WILL BE UNDER MY CONTROL.
THE BLOOD OF IRELAND WILL BE SPILT, HER RIVERS WILL RUN RED. NOBODY WILL STAND IN MY WAY, NOT EVEN THE GODDESS OF WAR.
KTHUNK

TAKE ME BACK TO MY FORT IN CRUACHÁN, MY PET.
QUICK, SHE MAY STILL BE ALIVE.
COUGH
YOU, BOY, COUGH, COME CLOSER.

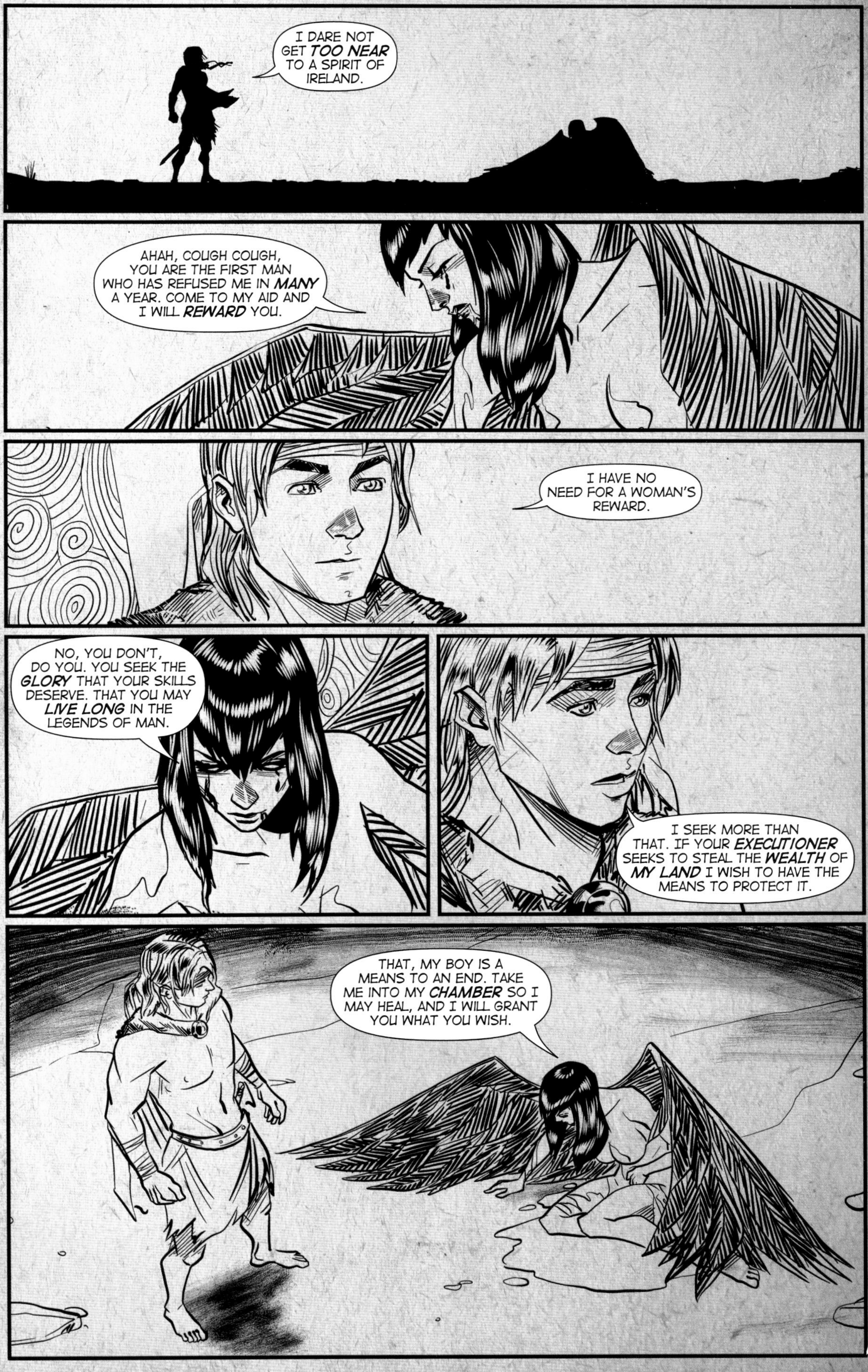

I DARE NOT GET ***TOO NEAR*** TO A SPIRIT OF IRELAND.

AHAH, COUGH COUGH, YOU ARE THE FIRST MAN WHO HAS REFUSED ME IN ***MANY*** A YEAR. COME TO MY AID AND I WILL ***REWARD*** YOU.

I HAVE NO NEED FOR A WOMAN'S REWARD.

NO, YOU DON'T, DO YOU. YOU SEEK THE ***GLORY*** THAT YOUR SKILLS DESERVE. THAT YOU MAY ***LIVE LONG*** IN THE LEGENDS OF MAN.

I SEEK MORE THAN THAT. IF YOUR ***EXECUTIONER*** SEEKS TO STEAL THE ***WEALTH*** OF ***MY LAND*** I WISH TO HAVE THE MEANS TO PROTECT IT.

IT IS LITTLE I WOULD CARE, IF MY LIFE WERE TO LAST ***ONE*** DAY AND ***ONE*** NIGHT ONLY, SO LONG AS MY NAME AND THE STORY OF WHAT I HAD DONE WOULD LIVE AFTER ME.

MORRIGAN. MY *GODDESS OF WAR*. YOU ONCE CALLED ME ARROGANT.

I SUPPOSE THE THOUGHT THAT I COULD RULE THIS LAND AHEAD OF ALL OTHERS WAS A BIT *GRANDIOSE*.

BUT LOOK NOW FROM YOUR GRAVE AT HOW THE KINGS OF IRELAND HAVE SACRIFICED THEIR OWN QUEENS FOR ME.

ARROGANT?, I THINK NOT.

POWERFUL, RUTHLESS, DETERMINED... THE GREATEST OF ALL QUEENS IN IRELAND.
EVEN THE MIGHTY FERGUS MAC RÓICH, SON OF THE GREAT HORSE, FOSTER FATHER OF THE VERY MAN WHO OPPOSES US.
YOU TOOK THE HEAD OF YOUR OWN WIFE, TO PROVE YOURSELF TO ME.

AND YOU, CORMAC CONNLOINGES,
SON OF THE GREAT CONCHOBAR MAC NESSA, THE KING OF THE ULAID, LEADER OF THE RED BRANCH ARMY, WHOSE DOMINION I SEEK TO TAKE FOR MY OWN.

YOU LEAD MY ARMY BLINDLY TO THEIR DEATHS. YOU WOULD GIVE YOUR LIFE FOR ME IN A HEARTBEAT.
MY HOLD OVER YOU IS UNBREAKABLE.

ARROGANT?

WE WILL SEE ABOUT THAT.

TAKE ME BACK TO MY CHARIOT.

'when the time for war comes, and my burial chamber fills with light,
'I will rise from my grave in a form unknown to you.'
'Be brave, my boy, for I will awaken to feast on your flesh.'
'I will be there by your side, as you die.'

Celtic Warrior

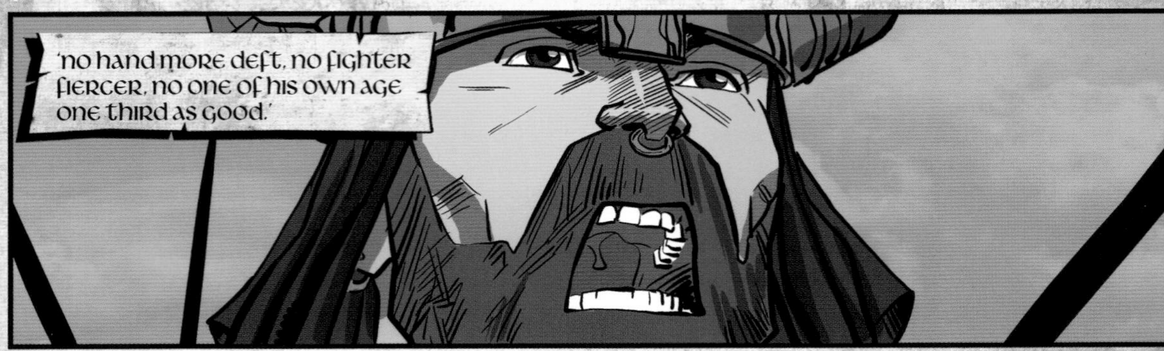

Cú Chulainn

chapter four

'no one can match his youth or vigour; for fame or form; for voice or strength or sternness;
for cleverness, courage or blows in battle; for fire or fury, victory, doom or turmoil.'

SKILL

HOLD THERE. I BRING SOME NEWS!
HAVE YOU DESERTED YOUR SCOUT PARTY, MAC ROTH?
NO, I HAVE NOT. MY COMPANIONS ARE DEAD. I BARELY MADE IT OUT WITH MY LIFE. IT IS AS IF THE COOLEY MOUNTAINS THEMSELVES TURNED ON US.
THEN IT APPEARS THAT TAKING THE PATH BY SEA IS OUR SAFEST OPTION AFTER ALL.
YOUR KING, FERGUS, HAS ALREADY LEFT, BUT YOU MAY SAIL WITH US. IT LOOKS LIKE WE WILL NEED ALL THE HELP WE CAN GET.
THIS IS NOT GOING TO BE AN EASY CROSSING.

HEAVVVVE,
HEAVE LIKE YOUR VERY LIFE DEPENDS ON IT.
HEAAAAVVE!
LOOK THERE. SHE'S GOING UNDER.
WE CANNOT TURN AROUND. KEEP ROWING OR WE WILL SUFFER THE SAME FATE.

WE SHOULD NEVER HAVE RISKED OUR LIVES IN THESE SEAS. LIR, THE GOD OF THE OCEAN IS AGAINST US. WE ARE FOOLS TO HA...
THE ISLE OF SKYE IS JUST UP AHEAD. WE CAN SHELTER FROM THE STORM. FOR MAEVE!!
FOR MAEVE!

BLUGGHH

WE ARE ON DRY LAND NOW, MY FRIEND. OUR JOURNEY IS ALMOST OVER.

WE CAN CROSS THE GIANT'S CAUSEWAY TO REACH OUR FOE.
HEH, I TAKE IT YOU DON'T BELIEVE IN GIANTS.

ASSEMBLE SOME OF YOUR BEST WARRIORS. WE ARE NOT SAFE THIS NIGHT YET.

THIS IS THE ISLAND OF THE SCATHACH. WE MUST GAIN HER PERMISSION BEFORE WE CAN LEAVE.

WHY NOT TAKE THE ISLAND BY FORCE? WE STILL HAVE OVER FIVE THOUSAND MEN.
KRAKOOOOOOM
BY ERIU'S GHOST!
WOULD YOU CARE TO ENLIGHTEN THE BOY, MY DEAR MAEVE, OR SHALL I?
THIS IS THE VERY TRAINING GROUND OF THE ONE YOU SEEK TO DESTROY.
TO REACH HIM, YOU MUST FIRST PROVE YOURSELF AGAINST ONE OF MY OWN.
SEND AS MANY AS YOU WISH, YOU FACE JUST ONE OPPONENT. THAT BRIDGE IS THE ONLY WAY THROUGH TO THE CAUSEWAY.

I FEAR **NO MAN**. WITH ME, MY BROTHERS.
LOOK THERE.
WHAT IN HELL?
THOOOOOOM

Four years ago.
IF YOU WISH TO PERFECT THE SALMON LEAP YOU MUST USE ALL OF YOUR BODY TO THRUST YOURSELF INTO THE AIR.
YOUR LEGS MUST KICK STRONGER THAN THE MIGHTIEST WAVE.
YOUR BODY MUST TWIST IN THE WIND AS IF IT IS GLIDING THROUGH THE MOST POWERFUL RIVER.
AND KEEP THAT CHISELLED JAW UP.
THAP
HEY!

IT'S NOT LOOKING SO CHISELLED NOW, IS IT?
HA, YOU'RE GOING TO REGRET THAT ONE, FERDIA.
HAHA, GET OFF ME, WILL YOU.
KTHUNK
ALL RIGHT, ALL RIGHT, I'M NOT GOING TO SHAPE YOU BOYS INTO THE FINEST WARRIORS IN IRELAND IF I LET YOU FIGHT EACH OTHER ALL DAY.
IT TAKES YEARS TO MASTER MY SKILLS. VERY FEW HAVE EVEN LEFT HERE WITH THEIR LIVES.

YOU MUST ENDURE THE HEROES' COIL ON THE SPIKES OF SPEARS.
CROSS THE PLAIN OF ILL LUCK.
SURVIVE A NIGHT IN THE PERILOUS GLENS
LEARN THE SPURT OF SPEED.
MASTER THE POISONED STROKE.

YOU WILL SING THE HEROES' SCREAM.
SO YOU CAN START BY KEEPING YOUR CHINS UP WHEN YOU ARE IN THE AIR. DO YOU BOYS THINK YOU CAN HANDLE THAT?
YOUR DESTINIES ARE INTERTWINED. THEY WILL BE SPOKEN OF IN THIS LAND FOR CENTURIES TO COME.

ONE OF YOU WILL HEAR THE ***WHITE HORNED BULL*** ROAR AGAINST THE ***BROWN BULL OF ULSTER***.

IT WILL COME WITH FORCE, SEEKING TO CLAIM YOUR HOMELAND AS ITS OWN.

IN THESE ***DARK GATHERINGS OF BLOOD***, THIS VERY SPEAR, THE ***GAE BOLGA***, THE ***SPEAR OF MORTAL PAIN***, WILL SEPARATE YOU TWO.

ATTACCCKK!
CTHAK
HNNNGH

THUUUMP
KLINNGH

KRAKOOOOOM
SHHLINNNTH

CHARGE ON THAT BRIDGE.

CRAACK

ONLY THE GAE BOLGA WILL SEPARATE THEM!

ENOUGH OF THIS.

AND ESPECIALLY NOT HIS ***WEAKER*** HALF--BROTHER.

YOU. ARE. MINE.

I'M CROSSING THE CAUSEWAY.
DO **NOT** EVEN THINK ABOUT **STOPPING** ME UNLESS YOU WANT THE SAME FATE FOR ALL YOUR PRECIOUS TRAINEES.
FOLLOW ME TO ULSTER. OUR VICTORY IS AT HAND.
MY DEAR **CÚ CHULAINN,** THE TIMES I HAVE TRAINED YOU FOR ARE HERE. THE **DARK GATHERINGS OF BLOOD** ARE UPON US,
I JUST HOPE YOU ARE READY, BECAUSE YOU HAVE **NO IDEA** WHAT YOU ARE UP AGAINST.

'his body made a furious twist inside his skin.'

the legend of Cú Chulainn

chapter five

'the light from the sun flickered red in the vapour that rose boiling above his head.'

BRAKOOOOM
'no fury more fierce. no power more strong. the battlefield ran red as the warp spasm took hold.'

knowledge

WHAT WAS THAT YOU SAID ABOUT GIANTS AGAIN?
BRAKOOOM

ONE YEAR AGO
I, CONALL CERNACH HAVE COME HERE TO CLAIM YOUR RICHES FOR BRICCRIU'S FEAST, SO THAT I MAY BE KNOWN AS THE MIGHTIEST WARRIOR OF IRELAND.
I, LŌEGAIRE BŪADACH HAVE COME HERE TO CLAIM YOUR RICHES FOR BRICCRIU'S FEAST, SO THAT I MAY BE KNOWN AS THE MIGHTIEST WARRIOR OF IRELAND.
JUST TELL US YOUR RIDDLE, GIANT.

MY RICHES ARE YOURS TO TAKE FREELY. TO DO SO YOU MUST PERFORM BUT ONE FEAT. I WILL LAY MY HEAD DOWN UPON MY BLOCK AND YOU SHALL CHOP IT FROM MY SHOULDERS. I ASK ONLY THAT IF I SURVIVE, YOU SHALL PLACE YOUR HEAD ON YOUR BLOCK SO THAT I MIGHT BRING MY AXE DOWN UPON MY OWN AFTERWARDS.
HAH! YOU THINK I AM NOT STRONG ENOUGH TO REMOVE YOUR HEAD FROM YOUR SHOULDERS.
THIS SWORD IS MADE FROM THE FINEST STEEL OF TARA, IT CAN CUT THROUGH ANYTHING.
THIS SWORD HAILS FROM LANDS ACROSS LIR'S OCEAN. IT HAS NEVER MET A NECK IT CANNOT SLASH RIGHT THROUGH.
WELL THEN, WHY NOT HAVE BOTH OF YOU TRY AT THE SAME TIME.

KSHUNK

HAHA, THE RICHES ARE OURS.

SURELY NOW ONE OF US SHALL BE THE ONE TO CUT THE CHAMPION'S PORTION WHEN WE DINE AT DUN RUDRAIGE.
THEY WILL SING SONGS OF US WHEN DRUNK ON WINE.

THE WOMEN WILL RECITE POETRY IN OUR NAMES.

EVEN THE MIGHTY...

AAAGHHHH!

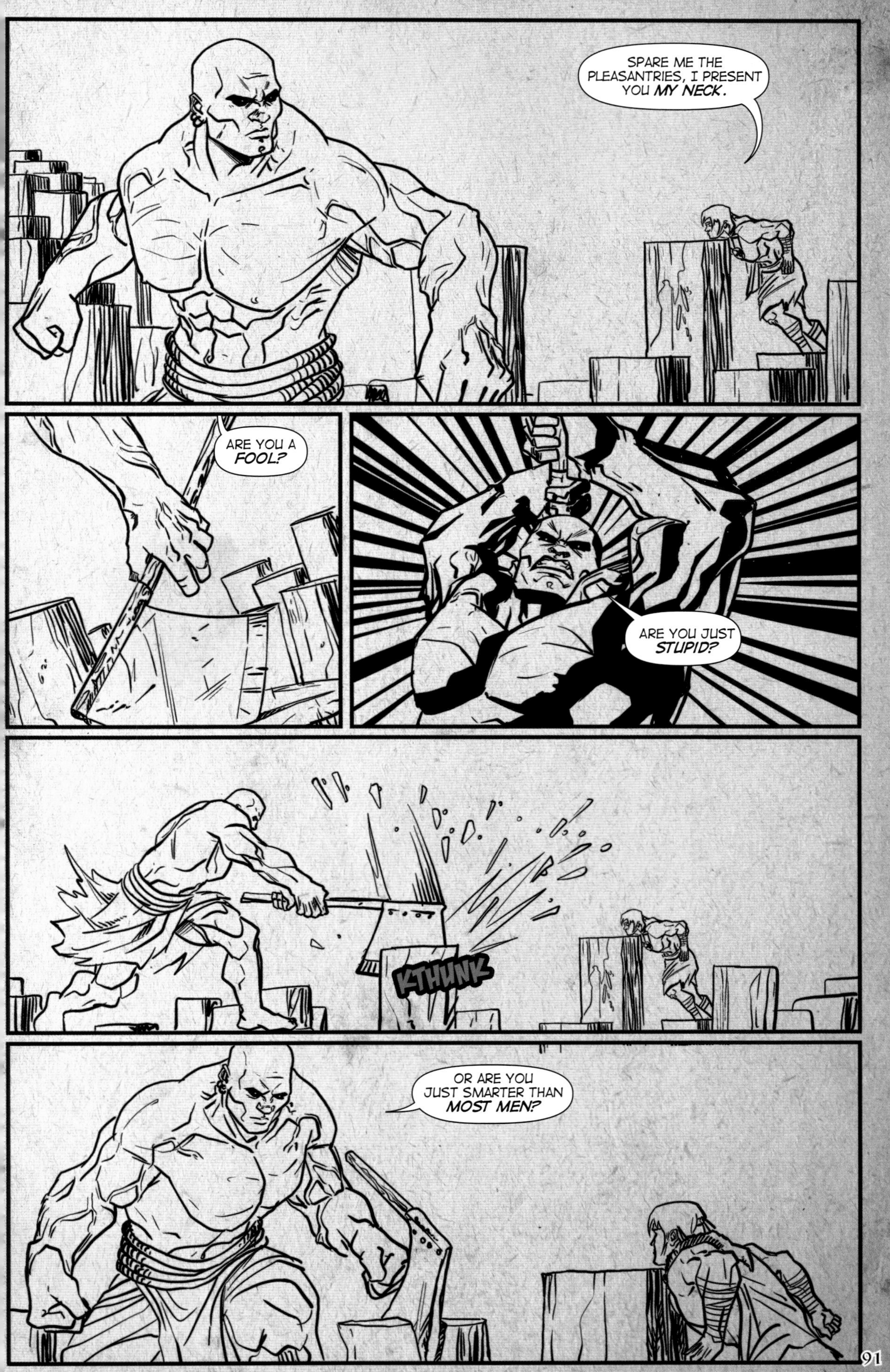
SPARE ME THE PLEASANTRIES, I PRESENT YOU MY NECK.
ARE YOU A FOOL?
ARE YOU JUST STUPID?
KTHUNK
OR ARE YOU JUST SMARTER THAN MOST MEN?

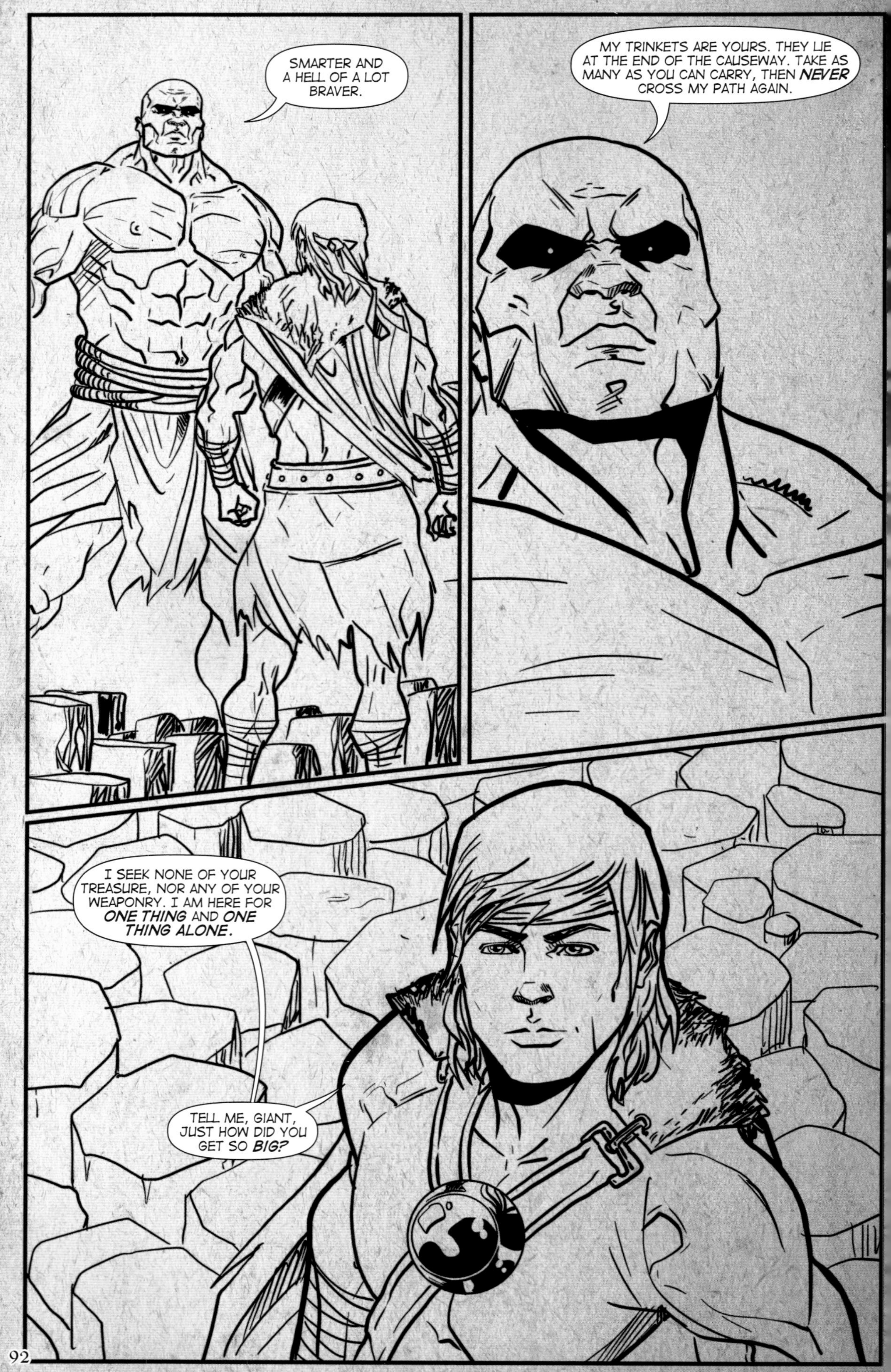
SMARTER AND A HELL OF A LOT BRAVER.
MY TRINKETS ARE YOURS. THEY LIE AT THE END OF THE CAUSEWAY. TAKE AS MANY AS YOU CAN CARRY, THEN NEVER CROSS MY PATH AGAIN.
I SEEK NONE OF YOUR TREASURE, NOR ANY OF YOUR WEAPONRY. I AM HERE FOR ONE THING AND ONE THING ALONE.
TELL ME, GIANT, JUST HOW DID YOU GET SO BIG?

RAAAAARRRRRGGHH.
THOOOM
HE IS ABOUT TO FALL. KEEP FIGHTING.
BRAKOOOM

AIM FOR HIS *EYES*.

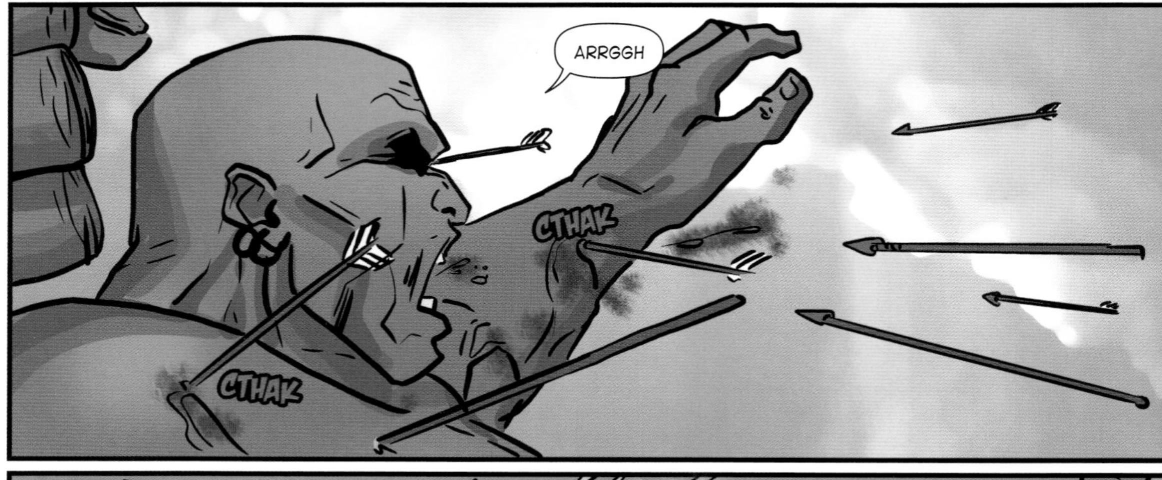
ARRGGH
CTHAK
CTHAK

THOOOM

FINALLY...
'the foot of the giant's causeway'
WE HAVE REACHED ULSTER.

IT LOOKS AS THOUGH THE RUMOURS WERE TRUE ABOUT THE MEN OF ULSTER BEING UNDER A CURSE.
IT MAKES YOU WONDER HOW BAD OUR HOMES ARE FARING AFTER WE DESERTED THEM ON THIS QUEST.
LOOK. HERE THEY ARE. INSIDE THEIR DWELLINGS, SOUND ASLEEP.
THEIR WOMEN, ON THE OTHER HAND!
NOOOO. LEAVE US IN PEACE
I THINK IT'S TIME WE TOOK A LITTLE MOMENT TO ENJOY OURSELVES AFTER OUR LONG JOURNEY.
KTHUNK
ACK!

CTHAK
CRAACK
THOOOM
WE ARE BEING TAKEN OUT BY A LONE SLINGSHOT. *PROTECT* THE QUEEN.

YOU FOOLS, GET INTO THE FOREST FOR COVER.
THOOOM
QUICKLY. MEN WILL NOT LAST LONG OUT HERE.

KEEP ON MOVING.
AIIEE!
CRAACK
IT'S... IT'S A TRAP!
OH NO, WE HAVE BEEN LED IN HERE ON PURPOSE.
THOOOM

SHLUMP
SHHLINNTH
WE NEED TO GET OUT OF HERE. HEAD FOR THAT CLEARING.

WHATEVER WAY YOU LOOK AT IT, WHATEVER EXTRAORDINARY SKILLS YOU POSSESS, IT IS STILL ONE THOUSAND MEN AGAINST ONE.
... THE BULL DONN CUAILNGE WILL FALL AND ULSTER WILL BE MINE!
NOT TODAY.

Celtic Warrior

the legend of Cú Chulainn

chapter six

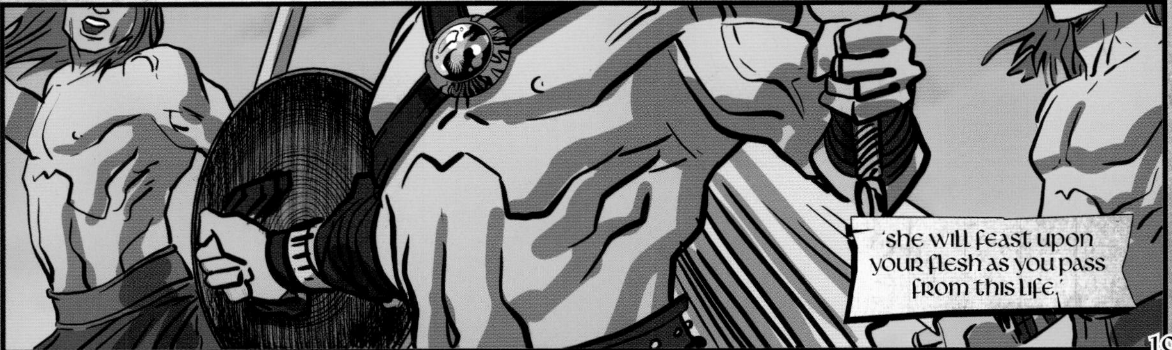

War

CTHAK

KILL HIM

CTHAK

THUUUMP

SHHLINNNTH

KILL HIM AND BRING ME THE BROWN BULL OF ULSTER.

CRAACK

IS THAT THE BEST YOU CAN DO?

BRAKOOOM

HE IS JUST ONE MAN!
WHAT THE...?
THOOOM
EVERYBODY, ATTACK HIM ALL AT ONCE. NOW!

BRAKOOOM
HEYEARRRGH!
RRRGGGGGHHHHHHHHHHEEAAA
AAAGGGGHHHHHHHHGGRRR
RAAAAAGGGHHHAAAAAAGGH
YOU WILL NEVER CONQUER THIS LAND.

NEVER!
THOOOM
YOU WERE RIGHT!
I AM BUT ONE MAN.
KTHUNK
ONE MAN WHO IS DEFEATING A WHOLE ARMY.
BORN NAMED SETANTA, RAISED AS THE HOUND OF CULAINN, GUARDIAN OF THIS ENTIRE LAND.
THERE IS NOBODY IN YOUR ARMY THAT CAN DEFEAT ME.
NOBODY?

NOT EVEN YOUR DEAR BROTHER, *FERDIA?*

NO...

IT CAN'T BE.

I KNEW MY ARMY COULDN'T DEFEAT YOU, CÚ CHULAINN. NO MATTER HOW MANY MEN I POSSESSED. THEY SERVED ONLY TO PROTECT ME AS I JOURNEYED ACROSS THE ISLAND.

YOU THINK THAT A GOD LIKE ME WOULD NOT SEE YOU SAVE MORRIGAN ON THAT NIGHT? YOU MADE A DEAL WITH THE GOD OF WAR, ONE THAT SAW YOU GAIN IMMUNITY FROM MY SEDUCTIONS.
SHE SAID NOTHING ABOUT THE ATTACKS OF YOUR FRIEND.

HYEEAAAH
FWOOSH
FERDIA, STOP.
KLINNGH
SHE HAS YOU *INTOXICATED*. YOU MUST BREAK FREE.
CRAACK
UUUGFFH

UNNGGH
CTHAK
KTHUNK
I CANNOT FIGHT YOU.
AGGHH
SHLUMP
THOOOM
I WON'T... I *WON'T KILL YOU*.

YOU...
YOU MUST.
CRAACK
NNGH
NO!
YOU HAVE TO STOP ME. OR ELSE ALL OF IRELAND WILL FALL TO THIS MAD WOMAN.

FWOOSH
NOO
SHHLINNNTH

I AM TRULY SORRY, MY FRIEND.
AAAARGH!
SHLIICCK

YOU HAVE FAILED, BOY. ULSTER WILL FALL. IRELAND WILL BE MINE.
NEVER.
UFF
JUST FALL DOWN AND DIE.

YOU WHAT?

YOU DARE TO CHALLEN....

FINE. I'LL DO IT MYSELF.
EVEN IN DEATH, YOU CONTINUE TO ANNOY ME CÚ CHULAINN.
AACCCKKK
SHHLINNNTH
YOU WILL NEVER, ENSLAVE THIS LAND. NO-ONE SHALL.

THOOOM
YOUR HOLD OVER THE MEN OF IRELAND HAS ENDED, WITCH.
KSHUNK

THE RED BRANCH HAVE AWOKEN. HER CURSE HAS COME TO AN END.
THOSE OF YOU LEFT STANDING. CHOOSE OF YOUR OWN FREE WILL. FIGHT FOR YOUR DEAD AND EVIL QUEEN,

OR HONOUR A MAN WHO STOOD BY HIMSELF IN DEFENCE OF HIS LAND.

WHO FOUGHT FOR US SO THAT EVERY GENERATION OF THE IRISH PEOPLE CAN ASSERT THEIR RIGHT TO FREEDOM AND SOVEREIGNTY.

WHOSE ACT OF COURAGE WILL BE KNOWN TO THE PEOPLE OF IRELAND FOREVER. A FAME THAT WILL INSPIRE ENDLESS GENERATIONS.

PEOPLE WILL DO ANYTHING TO DEFEND THEIR HOMES.

NO MATTER WHAT THE ODDS ARE.

ORDINARY MEN WILL STAND UP AGAINST EMPIRES.

YOUR DESCENDANTS WILL STAND BEFORE HIM IN AWE.

The Táin

The Táin Bó Cuailnge or the Cattle Raid of Cooley, on which the central story of *Celtic Warrior* is based, is one of the best known tales from a group of legends known as the Ulster Cycle. It tells of Queen Maeve (Medb) of Connacht's obsession to acquire the Brown Bull of Cooley, an animal noted for its strength and potency.

Probably originally in an oral form and passed down in storytelling from generation to generation, The Táin survives in written form in 12th century manuscripts in the Irish language and was translated into English by poet Thomas Kinsella in 1969, illustrated by Louis le Brocquy.

Legendary Ulster warrior Cú Chulainn is the hero of The Táin and in *Celtic Warrior* we also get flashbacks to his early life in the story of how, having been born Setanta, he acquired the name Cú Chulainn (Hound of Culainn); how he was rewarded by Morrigan, the godess of war, for saving her life, and how he acquired some of his extraordinary skills and supernatural abilities.

The image of Cú Chulainn on page 126 of the book, dying, but bound upright to a post so that he might face his enemies even in death, is that of the iconic bronze sculpture by Oliver Sheppard (1911) that stands in the central hall of the General Post Office (GPO) in O'Connell Street, Dublin.

WILL SLINEY is an award-winning, Cork based illustrator who has worked at the top level of illustration for years. He broke into the worldwide scene illustrating *Star Wars*, *Farscape* and *MacGyver* before working on the record-breaking Marvel comics series *Fearless Defenders*.

First published 2013 by The O'Brien Press Ltd.,
12 Terenure Road East,
Rathgar, Dublin 6, Ireland
Tel: +353 1 4923333
Fax: +353 1 4922777
E-mail: books@obrien.ie
www.obrien.ie
Reprinted 2013.

ISBN: 978-1-84717-338-6

A catalogue record for this title is available from The British Library

2 3 4 5 6 7 8 9 10
13 14 15 16 17 18 19 20

Printed and bound in Poland by Białostockie Zakłady Graficzne S.A.
The paper in this book is produced using pulp from managed forests